It's More Than Returns

It's More Than Returns

*Getting to the Heart
of Retirement Planning*

Annalee Leonard
Mainstay Financial Group

Published by Mainstay Financial Group, Inc., 2810 East
Cervantes Street, Pensacola, FL 32503 Phone: 850-437-3127
Fax: 850-437-3998

Printed in the United States of America

ISBN-13: 978-0-9858875-0-6
ISBN-10: 0985887508

This book is dedicated to my Daddy,
Mrs. Spinella, Sister Mary Benedict,
and my best friend
and confidant, Dr. Joan Connell.

Thanks to each of you and all of the people
I have helped over the years.

Annalee

Acknowledgments

There have been people in my life who have encouraged me and told me that I could do whatever I wanted to do. People who let me know that I had been given the gift of a good mind, and with that gift, I could help other people. I thank them with all of my heart, and I dedicate this book and all the years that went into getting me where I am now to them.

About the Author

nnalee Leonard specializes in working with retirees and those preparing to retire to preserve their assets and help ensure that their money lasts. The founder and president of Mainstay Financial Group, Annalee has offices in Pensacola, Florida, and Mobile, Alabama. She is licensed in insurance, investments, and long-term care solutions. Since 1990, Annalee has helped many of her clients lower their income taxes, reduce taxes on their Social Security income, and protect their estate values. She has helped many retirees increase their legacy with their Individual Retirement Accounts (IRAs) over multiple generations.

In 2009, Annalee was accepted into the nation's most exclusive group of financial advisors—Ed Slott's Elite IRA Advisor Group™. As a Master Elite IRA Advisor, Annalee is dedicated to solving the country's biggest and most complex financial problem—effectively managing the distribution of assets from IRAs.

Annalee is the host of her own radio show, "Winning with Annalee." The show airs on Tues-

Annalee with Beau, Jolie, and Bella.

day mornings from ten to eleven on WNRP News AM 1620.

Annalee has conducted hundreds of presentations on topics of interest to seniors, such as estate planning, fixed annuities, long-term care solutions, savings bonds, funeral trusts, retirement planning, and asset preservation. Through affiliation with several senior affinity groups, she presents a monthly program on a variety of financial topics relevant to seniors from Mobile, Alabama, to Port St. Joe, Florida.

A native of Louisiana, Annalee has resided in the Pensacola area since 1990. Her hobbies are golfing, enjoying the beach, travelling in her motor home, and caring for her "business partners" and office entertainers, Beau, Jolie, and Bella.

Preface

Are you facing retirement? Does estate planning bewilder and confuse you? Do you need help directing or managing your financial affairs?

Annalee Leonard can help you do more than invest your money. She is a heartfelt advisor who cares for your entire well-being.

Annalee's riveting story is the driving force of her career. After her father had died without any estate planning, her family shattered. Sadly, the greed of one brother destroyed the entire family unit. Since then, she has made it her personal mission to help other families avoid the terrible pain her family experienced.

Annalee is especially concerned for women, particularly widows who are easily intimidated by financial decision-making. Each of her clients is special to her, and she has some great stories to tell that demonstrate how preserving your future requires more than money.

This book may not give you all the answers, but it will give you some of the questions you need to ask about your financial affairs and estate. The intent of this book is to help you take the next step, to do something about what you learned so that you can win today and plan ahead so that your heirs are winners in the future, too.

Table of Contents

My Mission

I don't consider myself as having a job. I have a mission. I really do. I've been in the financial services business for over 23 years. I started at the bottom, a fact I carry as a badge of honor. I knocked on doors, selling health insurance, and then graduated to life insurance, finally moving to retirement planning for teachers using tax-shelter annuities. It is from there that I was able to establish my own practice doing complete estate planning.

I truly can say that I really, really love what I do. Every day, I make someone's life better, and I can make generations of lives better by dealing with that one person. That is something for which I am grateful. I also feel that it is a tremendous obligation because I have been given such an awesome blessing.

Many years before I was a financial planner, I was an educator. I carry that experience into what I do today: I teach, I solve problems, and I work with a team. I very much believe in a team approach. I have attorneys and CPAs on the same page. I don't want to do their job, and I also don't want them doing my job. We work together on behalf of our clients.

I'm constantly learning, going to classes, speaking with people who know more than I do, and sharing knowledge. My purpose for this is twofold. I make myself a better advisor, and then I also mentor women coming into this business. I want them to be the best that they can be.

I think many people see the financial industry as a place where they are going to make a very good living, and that is all they see. They take a test, get a license, and think they know everything that there is to know. They take what additional education is required to keep their license, and that's the end of it. Most of those people don't last very long, thank goodness.

I have a mission, and I'm really, really passionate about it. My mission is to educate people and to help them, and their families, prevent what happened to my family. Lack of planning and not putting things in writing destroyed my family. It happened to my family, and I have seen it happen to other families who have come to work with me after the fact. It doesn't have to be this way. If you learn how to make smart financial decisions, your family can avoid much of the grief that occurs after your death.

My goal is to help people move off square one and start doing something about their finances and their estate. I am not a pushy person, but I am determined to get the message out. I see what I do as a service. I am always blunt and honest because I am concerned. I am here to serve the people who come into my office. If I am truly serving you, I am going to make sure your entire financial situation is healthy. Part of that is making sure you have a good attorney, making sure your estate planning is done, making sure nobody is taking advantage of you.

I treat everybody with the same respect and try to help people learn how to make the right decisions for themselves so they can make their lives better. I don't demand trust from my clients; I consider it a privilege when I earn it. This book is my humble attempt to convey this passion and mission I've been living for decades. I hope that, through the stories and experiences of some of my dear clients, you'll come to see who I am and determine whether your values line up with mine. I trust this short book will be well worth the time and attention you give it!

Ready or Not

Retirement eventually happens. Death eventually happens. What all of us have in common, no matter what our age, our gender, or nationality, is that there will be a day when we will not be going to work again, and there will be a day when we die.

There are times when illnesses come into our lives for which we haven't planned and for which we are not prepared. That's the nature of illness. People can go through a separation or a divorce after many years of marriage, and they can be blindsided by it. We don't plan for these things.

So we have to plan for the things that we know are coming and prepare for the unexpected. These are the truths we face in life. Are you ready for this?

People often say, "I don't have enough money to worry about it." Well, if you have anything at all and you have people you love, then you have an estate. You *need* to worry about the things that you have. Will these things go to the people that you love without causing unnecessary cost and strife? Are the people you love going to be taken care of? Have you left them in a position where things are organized, or will you leave things in such a mess or so misunderstood that nothing is ever touched, and it all just deteriorates? Ready or not, these are the questions you need to ask yourself. I am here to help you find the answers.

Protecting Your
Nest Egg

One of my favorite things is to see the osprey in the spring. The male and female ospreys participate in building an unbelievably huge nest, and once the eggs are laid, one of the parents is always there for protection.

That is what you have to do with your nest egg. You've spent a lot of time building your nest and creating your nest egg. Now you have to protect it. One of the things you need to be aware of is that there can be some awfully large cracks in your nest egg.

One of the first cracks usually is your estate plan. No matter how much money you have, if you don't have a plan, somebody else is going to plan for you. It's either going to be the state or it's going to be your family, and there will be controversy; they may go after each other, and what you wanted won't matter. These are the harsh but very real facts of life

My mission started many years ago when my father died. Daddy's death was very, very unexpected. He was a very smart man, but he wasn't an educated man. Like many people from his era, he left high school early. He helped his mom with the other children. He went to war. He got his GED the same year I graduated high school; we used to hang our diplomas side by side.

He thought having a will made everything

fine, but my father died before my mother did, so we had an unbelievable controversy that started within an hour of my father's death. Who was going to run the family now? Who was going to make the decisions? It started right away, and you could see the grief factor starting to settle in immediately. Daddy left a simple will saying how things were to be distributed, and of course, everything went to my mother and then to the children. My mom's will was a duplicate of his. The day before my mother died, her will was changed. Because of that action, four of us have spent 23 years not talking to each other. It was just recently, on Christmas Eve, when I finally spoke to my youngest brother, and I found out the truth of everything that had gone on. He was told lies about me, and I was told lies about him, by the person who wound up getting everything. It was so terrible. Our family had just disinte-grated. We can never replace the years that were stolen from us.

I can't tell you how devastating that was, to go through the biggest loss of my life, the loss of a parent, and then all of a sudden lose my family at the same time. If I can help your family avoid going through that—if I can help you keep your family intact and talking to each other and working as a unit—then I have done what I've been put here to do.

A healthy financial plan includes the estate planning that goes with it. One of the biggest failures that I've seen in my 23 years in the financial services industry is that many so-called planners help people put their money in stocks and mutual funds and send them home. They seldom go that step further to make sure that the estate is in good order.

What would happen if you died tomorrow? That's the question I ask my clients. For example, I recently had a client who had over $4,000,000, and he wanted me to start working with him to invest it. We started talking, and it turned out he's in a second marriage (both had children from their previous mar-riages), his wife is much younger, he has a special-needs child, runs a business, owns multiple pieces of property, and he did not even have a will. If he had died suddenly, his second wife would have been on the streets, all of the aid his daughter was receiving would be gone and she would have run through her share of the money very quickly and then have nothing. He had no idea.

I gave him the names of several good attor-neys. I told him what to talk to them about, and that I would help them pull together a plan for him and his family. He now has a trust for himself, and he set up a special trust for his present wife that made sure she would always have a place to live. He has a special-needs trust for the daughter, and he has set money aside for the present wife. By building a plan, he has ensured the two sets of children will not have to bicker after the deaths of their parents.

Can you imagine what would happen if he had died without this planning? This man had money in the major financial houses, but there was no planning involved. This shows how everyone should be educated about money. Everyone needs to have somebody hold their hand and review their plan every couple of years to make sure it is still performing as needed.

What do you want to happen if you die? Do you want the daughter in law (whom you may not even like) to get the estate if your son passed away? Do you want your grandchild to get it? There are so many things to consider— even simple things such as U.S. Savings Bonds can cause a probate situation if they are not titled properly. Do you want to disinherit the people you love? Unless you want Uncle Sam to get the majority of your nest egg, you need a plan.

All About Risk

Another crack in your nest egg is risk that is not being adequately managed. It seems to me that the days of buying and holding are dead and gone. That used to be a good philosophy when there was more stability in the market. It just doesn't seem to be like that anymore. Just think about it for a minute. In days gone by, when something happened in Europe, it took three weeks before you knew about it. Now something happens in the Far East, and we know about it immediately. As it is happening, we are watching it. Within a nanosecond, those things affect what goes on in the market.

If you're thinking about putting money at risk, consider the ups and downs that occur. After a substantial loss, do you have time to wait for money to regain? How old are you? Will you still be here when the market does come back? Do you need the money to live the way you want to live today?

Think about it this way: there are three stages in the lifecycle of money. These are:

- Accumulation
- Preservation
- Distribution

The accumulation stage occurs when you are working and saving. During that period, you normally can assume more risk in hopes of greater returns because you are younger, earning a salary, and hopefully saving money.

Then you enter the preservation stage. That begins in your late fifties and into your seventies. You have to preserve what you've accumulated. Think of how many years it took you to put the money together. If you lose $30–$40,000, it means so much more because you are running out of time. Recently, a couple came to me; they had lost over $100,000 with their broker over a three-year period. They started with $340,000 in the beginning. They suffered a 29% downturn, and a 29% rebound only gets them back to $309,600; this is the cruel math of the marketplace. How many years did it take them to make $100,000? How much work? How much sweat and tears?

Please don't buy into this idea that it's only paper, that it's not a loss until you sell it. When the market is good it is easy for people to say, "Look what I earned." When it goes the other way, they write it off saying it was only paper. What is money made out of? This is real! This is what you put your life into.

You should want to preserve what you earned and still get decent growth. Notice the term I used, "decent growth." I'm not saying to stay stagnant. Get decent growth while preserving what you have. At the preservation stage, you are not taking the risk required to achieve 30–40% returns. When you shoot for growth that high, remember how far down you can drop. It can be cruel. If you go down 30%, you don't have to come back 30% to be even, you have to come back 43% to break even.

The next stage is distribution, when you want to start using some of your money. This is the retirement stage; you've got to plan for this. You can't just start taking money out while saying, "Oh, I'll make it back. I won't touch my principal again for a while." This is when you have to work a disciplined plan, just as disciplined as was the accumulation phase. The people who don't have a plan are the people who run out of money.

I have seen this happen way too often with potential clients who have not been guided properly in the past. I have seen people taking 20 and 30% each year from an account that is losing money, and no one has told them how quickly the nest egg will run out. You have to plan for accumulation, and you have to plan for preservation. Then you have to plan for rational distribution and legacy, or estate planning, because, if you do this right, you will have an estate to distribute when you are gone, and you will have lived your life to the fullest.

There Are Safe Places
to Invest Your Money

There are two places you can put your money: places that are safe, protected, and guaranteed, or places that are at risk. That's it.

What are protected and guaranteed? CDs, U.S. Savings Bonds, treasury certificates, bank accounts, fixed annuities, and life insurance cash value. These are boring, plain vanilla investments. They are not exciting, but they are safe. Whole life insurance is so overlooked for younger people. If done properly, you loan yourself money later in life from your policy, and it's tax-free. For younger people, these often are the best tools to use to help plan for a child's education, to pay a home off later, to help in retirement. This can turn into a stream of income when you are older that never has to be paid back; the death benefit is just less.

Once you get to a certain age, you've got to stop playing the game of catch up. People are living longer, and some of us are working longer, so you have to look for things that are going to give you "sleep insurance" so you don't have to worry and can sleep well at night.

Look at how much risk you really have in each type of investment. Where there is great potential for growth, there also is the opportunity for great loss. Be familiar with the pyramid of risk. There are some areas where people should not venture—those who can't afford to lose the money shouldn't be there. Bonds—not U.S. Savings Bonds—also have a degree of risk. You might think placing 50% in bonds and 50% in the stock market makes for a balanced portfolio. Unfortunately, bonds and stocks both have risks. Mutual funds and variable annuities have less risk, but there still is risk involved. In variable annuities, you can buy a guaranteed return, you can buy guaranteed income, and you can buy a death benefit, but you still are subject to market fluctuations. No matter how you dress it up, there is risk. Real estate, too, is cyclical. Look at where we are today: some homes are worth 20–50% less than when they were purchased.

Ask yourself how much of your money you can afford to lose. Write it down on a piece of paper in front of you so you can see it. You can be as risky as you want with that money **if** it will not affect your lifestyle now or later.

Another way to look at your risk ability is

the rule of 100: if you are 60, you should have no more than 40% of your money at risk. If you are 70, no more than 30% of your money should be at risk. I am not saying you must have it at risk, you should have **no more** than that amount of money at risk, and it seems to me that it should be managed risk. You may want to consider having someone who understands money watching this for you. You also should have true diversification. This doesn't mean having accounts in five different places. Real diversification is having enough spread in what you have so that if one part of the market goes down, you have other parts to support you.

Your first enemy is time. We all run out of time. The other enemy you have is the market and what it does. Did you ever notice the animals that represent the market? Bulls and bears. They are ferocious animals. They exist by destroying something else, and that is what the market is made of. It can be a cruel place.

If you look back in history to the Roaring Twenties, everything went flat after the stock market crash, didn't it? The same thing happened when the tech bubble and the real estate bubble burst. Everything went flat. You've got to be prepared. You've got to work in a way that if and when bubbles occur, you can weather the storm.

So how do you bulletproof your nest egg? Have a plan, build in safety. Having assets arranged so that you don't have to take money from an account that is down helps you to stretch your assets. Consider some of the better products that provide income that you cannot outlive and build in another stream of income for yourself. Have someone watching the at-risk money for you, and build in true diversification.

Dealing with Taxes

People always ask if they can evade paying taxes. There are two things I cannot help you evade: death and taxes.

I believe in paying taxes. I believe that we live in the best country in the world where we have more opportunity than anywhere else, so I pay my fair share, but no more.

Avoiding taxes is legal. If I want to go a few miles out of my way to avoid going across a toll bridge, that's legal. If I go speeding through the tollbooth and don't pay, that's evasion, and that is illegal. So, I can help you learn how to avoid paying more taxes than necessary, but never how to evade them. We only want to do what is legal.

Every firm should have as part of the team a CPA strategist who can help with tax matters. I am not a tax person; I'm a financial person. So I will bring in tax people to help us analyze your situation. I also am not an attorney, so I work with the best attorneys I can find so that you can take advantage of a team. Be very careful of some of the people who are out there doing legal work without a license—insurance agents should not be preparing your trust. Be careful of the low-cost trust—there is a reason it has a low cost; it may not be worth anything.

Many people are paying too much in taxes and are not prepared for what is coming when tax brackets change again in 2013. I don't have a crystal ball, but it looks as if they will increase. What are you doing to prepare for that?

Today, Roth IRAs often provide a great opportunity for you. No matter how much you make/earn, you can take a traditional IRA and convert it to a Roth IRA. Is this the right thing for you to do? I don't know unless we sit down and do an analysis, but this could be a tremendous way to pay taxes today when they are lower rather than paying taxes later when they are higher. Just think of this: If you wanted a car and had the money and you could buy that new car today for $10,000 or wait until 2013 when the same car will cost you $18,000, what would you do, all other things being equal? That's what you're looking at with a Roth IRA. You pay at today's tax rate.

There are no words more beautiful than tax-free. Perhaps you might want to look at investing in things that will be tax-free in the future, like Roth IRAs and life-insurance policies. If you are in a high enough tax bracket, one of the other things to consider is laddering, using tax-deferred fixed annuities to avoid paying taxes on money you are not using for current consumption. When you put money in a savings account, CDs, or the market—all of those things pay you interest, and at the end of the year, you get a 1099. Are you using that money? Then why are you paying taxes on it? Sometimes a bit of rearranging can help you lower your tax bracket and avoid paying taxes on your Social Security. One of the most important things I teach people is how to set up IRAs as a legacy for their heirs so that they literally stretch through generations. Again, I believe in paying taxes, but not more than necessary. For example, let's take a look at the case of a client we will call Doris. She died at 68. She left $250,000 in an IRA earning 7% to four different beneficiaries, $62,500 each for her son Frank, aged 33, two grandchildren, aged six and eight who split their portion, her daughter Peggy, aged 37, and another daughter Ann, aged 41. Before Doris's death, we set up a legal procedure called a stretch IRA.

Frank's portion, if he takes it across his lifetime and averages a 7% return, will distribute $492,731. The grandchildren's portion, working under the same assumption, will distribute over a million dollars. Peggy's portion will distribute $388,000. Ann, the older daughter, took her portion and paid the 30% tax on it and bought a car. That was the end of her inheritance. Which legacy would you rather leave your children? I would give anything if every year I got a check that said "for the benefit of Annalee Leonard, beneficiary of Lincoln A. Leonard." I would not care if that check was only for $50; that would be my most precious money of the year. This is what you leave: you leave a legacy. You leave them money. And if the heirs are smart and they're taught well, they're going to take the money they have to take out every year, pay the taxes on that, and reinvest it. When they get to be 65 or 70, they will then have two streams of income—one from your IRA and one from the reinvested money that also originally came from your IRA. You have built in an unbelievable retirement system for your children and grandchildren; what a great gift.

There are many good tools that you can use to hold money for future income for yourself or just leave it alone until you pass it on to other people, if you want to do that. You can set up an income that you can never outlive. Income riders allow you to start and stop your income; at the end, any remaining money goes to your heirs. Good, safe annuities can be freed up if you have a terminal illness or go into a nursing home. There are also instruments that provide dual purposes for long-term care protection and life insurance all in one. How much better can you get? If you need it, it's there for long-term care. If you don't use it, it goes to your heirs tax-free.

With so many options and variables, it is very difficult to know what to do. A good financial advisor can help you learn about and select the options that will help you best achieve your goals for your money and your family.

Choosing Your Lifestyle and Living Your Life!

How long is your money going to last? Why is this important? I told you about my father. He died at age 64. He and my mother referred to themselves as "old people." If somebody called me that today, I would be upset. Every day, I see people who are 80, 90, and even 100 years old living full and happy lives. A few years ago, one of my very good friends lost an aunt. Anne Frances was 100, and the joke was (it actually was the truth) if you wanted to remember something, tell Aunt Frances. The woman was just amazing.

We are living longer, and we are living more active lives. People used to retire, sit on the porch, and rock. Now when people retire, they are out there climbing rocks. There is a huge difference in our mentality and medicines. Things that were fatal not long ago are now curable. We have to take that into consideration. We are living longer. How do you want to live?

I have worked with people who don't have great resources, who deny themselves a better lifestyle because they want to leave money to their children. I tell them that their child is not my client, they are. If you are not allowing yourself to go out to eat with your friends or enjoy a trip you have always wanted to take—and you've got the money to do it—please reconsider. Don't trap yourself behind the closed doors of your house because you wish to leave your heirs thousands of dollars.

You have the freedom to actually go and live your life. Each individual makes his or her own decisions. I have clients now whose kids are making three times the amount of money their parents ever made. They usually don't need or even want their parents' money, but the parents often carry an unnecessary burden believing they have to leave money for their children. If you want to do that, that is your decision, but let's do it properly. The kids themselves usually want their mom or dad to enjoy life and not give up certain things just to leave an inheritance. I'm sure there are children who are not that way, but for the most part they are. If the kids don't need or don't want the money, you need to know that and act wisely to use it for yourself.

On Working
with Women

Because of the age group of many of my clients, I work with many women. Husbands have either passed away or are no longer able to handle financial affairs. Sometimes, they've been to another financial advisor whose only concern was how much money they had, and they were given a plan with very little consultation. Unfortunately, by the time some of these women get to me, they have unnecessarily lost tens of thousands of dollars. This is not an unusual scenario.

I also work with couples where the husband wants his wife to have someone she can come to if he dies first, someone she can believe in and trust. I always include the woman in the conversation. Too often, financial planners act as though the woman doesn't exist; sometimes, she's not even spoken to.

Women are still not treated as equal and able to understand what is going on. One of the things I tell women who visit me is that I don't expect them to know what I know. But if I were a brain surgeon, and I was going to operate on your brain, I'd want you to at least understand the basics of what I was going to do and the possible consequences. I wouldn't want you to do the surgery, but you've got to understand the basics; that way, you know why I recommend what I recommend. In this way, you don't become a person who just sits there, you become an active participant in your financial world.

A couple once came to see me, and after we had spoken for about 30 minutes, the husband looked at his wife and said, "We've found what we're looking for." When I asked him what he meant, he told me that, for that half hour, he was watching to see if I would bring his wife into the conversation, if I was going to speak with her and treat her with respect. He explained how they had met with an individual at a brokerage firm. While his wife was sitting right there, the planner looked at the husband and asked what his wife thought about the discussion. At that point, she got up and walked out.

Sometimes I almost have to force a wife to talk if she isn't participating. If we're discussing matters and she's just sitting there, I will look at her and say, "Tell me what you think. Tell me how you feel about this. Does this frighten you? Does this make you feel comfortable?"

The reality of life is that, most of the time, it's the wife who is the surviving spouse. If her husband were to die next week, she needs to know as much as he does about what to do and how to do it. Couples love this because most of the time it's the first time someone has addressed both of them with these questions. Too often one has been either talked down to or totally ignored during meetings.

Couples are very happy, and they are relieved by this level of communication. The husbands often tell me how they have tried to get their spouse involved in the planning process and start understanding it. Now we can work as a team and pull together what both parties want.

You are in a partnership and have built your money together. I don't care whether one has worked or both have worked; you've built it together, and, therefore, you both should be part of the financial decision-making. What fears do each of you have? We all know that the male psyche tends to be a little more aggressive and take more risk, but how does the wife really feel about risk? What is it doing to her stomach? Is she staying up at night because she's worried?

There always is some fear on both sides. The husband usually is playing the provider role and trying to provide security. He usually is not as confident as he is trying to appear because he really doesn't understand everything but doesn't want to let his wife know so that she doesn't worry. I actually am letting him off the hook by including his wife in the dialogue and the decision-making. We make every attempt to educate and alleviate their fears by getting both to a place of comfort. I answer all of their questions honestly and help them both make good decisions about their money.

Every day I get people who come to my office who have lost a spouse who took care of everything, and now they don't know what to do. They forget that marriage is supposed to be a partnership, and everything has to be worked out together, especially regarding the final plans each wants.

Financial decision-making requires a team approach. My job is to create a safe place for people to come together and work things out as a team, so when one member of the team is gone, the rest of the team knows what is supposed to be happening.

Selecting an Advisor

Mainstay Financial Group is an independent firm. When you work with us, we are able to investigate and offer an array of financial products that are available. Captive agents usually are not able to offer as much choice. It is like having a shoe salesman trying to put size five and a half shoes on every foot. For me, size five and a half is very comfortable, but for some, it would be too big, and for others, it would be too small.

Captive agents work with what they have and try to make it fit your situation. That also happens at banks and savings and loans because often they can only offer a small selection of financial products. In other words, we don't believe that everyone wears a size five and a half.

Whatever decision you make regarding the selection of an advisor, I encourage you to get a second opinion. At Mainstay, it won't cost you anything. Ultimately, you want somebody with whom you can sit down, look each other in the eye, and talk with openly and honestly. You should ask yourself if you are comfortable when you first go in. Do you feel stiff? Do you feel pressured? How do you *feel*? How you feel is important because dealing with money is emotional. Think about what happens when you lose money. Think about what happens when you make a major purchase. You get this unbelievable churning in your stomach, and your head spins, and your mouth gets dry.

That is not an intellectual response. That is an emotional response.

Women often come to me after their husband has passed away and they are scared to death. By the time we've talked ten or fifteen minutes, you can see their shoulders relax. You watch them start to smile. Their eyes soften because they're starting to have that feeling of comfort. You have to have that.

You need someone who's going to take the time to work with you, someone to help you understand why you're doing what you're doing, someone who is willing to educate you whether it takes two times, three times, or however many times it takes to go over the information. If you're walking out of a place, thinking you don't know what you just did, and are just hoping they're doing the right thing, you probably are doing the wrong thing.

I had a woman visit me this last week. An advisor had invested her money, but she didn't understand any of it and had no idea what fees she was being charged. I looked at her prospectuses and showed her where the fees were. All of her money was sitting in a fixed account making 3%, and her fees were almost 2%. Her advisor was telling her the money was safe, but he didn't tell her it was being eaten up with fees. It wasn't rational, and it wasn't fair to her.

When you are my client, we go through your plan step by step. We go through the pros and cons, and take the time to ensure you understand the financial products being used and the fees being charged. I don't expect you to become an expert, but I do want you to at least understand the basics, your options, and what you can expect. That's how I discuss financial health.

About Fees

Most people understand that nothing is free and that everybody has to make a living. When it comes to financial services, you need to understand the fees you are being charged and also know that you are not being double-charged. I've had so many people tell me that they have been with their advisor for many years and still don't understand how they are being charged. What kind of relationship is that?

There are basically three types of fees: commission-based fees, fee-based services, and consulting fees. The actual fees you are charged will depend upon a number of factors, including the principles of your advisor.

Commission-based fees are paid by the companies that provide financial products, including long-term care, life insurance, annuities, and Medicare supplements. You should not be charged any additional fees for these products. This payment comes from the general account of the company; it does not come from your money.

Fee-based services include retirement planning and portfolio management. Depending on the services provided, the fee might be an hourly rate or it could be an ongoing fee. If your plan includes the market, and I manage that money, there is a set fee, which is shown in writing. Fees should be discussed up front, and ongoing fees are deducted from your account. In our practice, you can see the fees every quarter on your statement. It is all very transparent, in black and white. Consulting fees are usually done on an hourly basis. Some advisors charge fees for their time just as an attorney would do. Be sure you understand what your advisor charges and why.

My Approach to Working with You

Have you ever sat down with an advisor and the first question out of his or her mouth is, "How much money do you have?" That's not appropriate. If they don't really want to know about you, your wishes, goals, and dreams, you need to get up and walk out of the door.

Financial services should be about protecting your interests and the interests of your children and grandchildren. Financial services also should be about education. I can't talk to a client without a blank sheet of paper and a pen so I can draw diagrams and write notes. People need to see and touch and own their financial situation. I don't want anyone walking out of my door wondering what they just did. I want you to know what you did and feel good about it so you can go home and sleep well. I want you to know and understand your plan, and if you have a question or don't remember something, I want you to know I will explain it again and again and again until you do.

I try to show people how wealth, health, and freedom tie in together. If you have a good handle on your wealth and you become ill, you won't be worried about having money to get care and medicine. When you have your wealth, you have the freedom to do things that you want to do.

Before we even meet, I will send you a letter and provide you with a list of the things that you need to bring with you to our first meeting. I don't want to waste your time or mine.

When we meet, I'm going to ask you many questions and will want you to tell me honestly about everything that is happening in your life. I've got to know all the pieces of the puzzle. People often wonder what difference some facts make. My job is to take care of you while you are alive and to take care of your heirs if you pass away. So, if I don't have all of the facts, I cannot do my job.

It all ties together. I need to know about you. I need to know about your family. I need to know about the dynamics of your family. Are we dealing with second marriages or third marriages? Do you have mixed families? Do you have kids from each side? How do they get along? How do they feel about the fact that you got married again? Do they like you? How do the kids communicate? I want to know about your dreams and your hopes. I want to know about your grandchildren and what you want for them. All of that information is going to become part of your plan. Without knowing all this private and personal information, I cannot make valid recommendations. I don't care if all you have is a checking account and a savings account, you still want all those things protected and left in the right way.

Don't come to me if you're not going to talk to me. I've had people try that. They come to me and say, "Tell me what you have." How can I tell them what I have when I don't know what they need? It would be like going to the car dealer who has every possible make of car on their car lot and you walk in and say, "I want a car." We need to be specific. We have to look at the reality of your life.

When you come in, I will start putting together a whole picture of you and your financial health. This includes tax returns, wills, power of attorney, and your medical power of attorney. How is your health? Do you have insurance policies? What is your income? How much risk are you willing to take with money? We will talk about your kids and grandkids. All of these things are very important to your financial health and well-being, so we review these upfront. I'm not a CPA, and I'm not an attorney, but I can look at these things and identify red flags and help you decide if you need to go to your attorney or CPA and have them review some facts.

Money is the last thing we will talk about. In my office, it doesn't matter if you have $40,000, $400,000, or $4,000,000. Money is relative. That $40,000 is just as important to that person as the $400,000 is to the other person. Each person is treated with the same dignity and the same concern. There are places out there now that if you walk in with less than $500,000, you don't even get to speak with a representative. You get whoever answers the phone or whoever is there that day. That is no way to be treated, and that's not how we do business.

The first visit takes about an hour and a half to go through everything. Of course, during that time you also ask me questions. It's important to ask those questions. You need to know what I do. You need to know about my fees. You need to know why I made that decision many years ago to be an independent rather than work for anyone other than my clients. We go through all of those things. At the end, I pull together what you have told me to make sure that I have heard everything correctly. We make sure that we're on the same page before you leave.

In the second meeting, I'm going to give you a plan. We will go over it step by step. After that second meeting, I will send you home to review what we discussed. If you have a question, write it down. If something concerns you, highlight it. If you want to involve your kids in the discussion, we will get them on the phone for a conference call. I don't expect you to interpret this process for them; it would be like me trying to interpret a doctor's diagnosis and treatment details to someone else.

On the third meeting, you're going to tell me what you like and don't like about the plan. We then will start to implement parts of the plan. Some plans are very simple to implement, but usually it becomes an ongoing process.

Once your plan is in place, we will review it on a regular basis. Things change, and as things change your plan needs to change too.

On Trust

To be successful working together, we have to be able to trust each other. You have to be able to trust me with your personal information and finances, and I have to be able to trust you to be honest about your situation. I am not going to share your private matters with anyone else unless you specifically want that. If you want your kids to join the conversation, that's fine with me. If you don't want your kids to know about your finances, they're not going to find out from me.

Once we have a plan put together, I will tell you to take it home with the understanding that you can see other estate planners and ask them what they would do. Let them give you their ideas; just don't give them my ideas. Planning is a valuable service that I provide you for free, but this process is a two-way street. I have to be able to trust you, and if I can't trust you not to take my work and give it to somebody else, then we really can't work together. We've got to trust each other. I truly feel that people appreciate when someone is talking to them as an equal, is willing to educate them, and is willing to trust them. That's what people should reasonably expect from a professional.

Sometimes, clients come in with things that need to be done and ask what they owe me. They don't owe me anything; they're my clients. I feel I owe that to them. If I have a client who passes away, I will sit with the spouse or the family and help them through the necessary paperwork. I don't charge them for that. That to me is the last thing that I can do for my client. And I do it out of respect for my client.

Clients are friends. Some of them become almost like family. We have one couple who often bring us homemade goodies just because they appreciate us; their kids say to them that we are like part of the family. I have clients who have been at my house for Christmas dinner. I've had some of the most wonderful people in the world in my office. I've had the privilege of serving people who have given me so much just by their presence, by their knowledge of life, by their outlook on life. I attend their funeral services. I'm a good Southern woman, and I tend to be very emotional. I cry like everybody else does because I am going to miss them terribly.

I'm also very particular about whom I work with. If somebody is a negative person, if somebody is going to come in and tell me how to do my job, I don't want to work with them. I don't surround myself with negativity or rudeness; I don't work that way, and I don't want to be around anybody else who does.

I desire to have a long-term relationship with my clients that it is for mutual benefit. I want to look out for your interests. I am not just a businessperson; I am your trusted advisor and even your friend because I am often looking after your entire livelihood and security. That is why trust is such a big deal for me.

Some of My Stories

In this chapter, you'll meet a few of my clients and hear about what I was able to do to tailor a plan for them.

Luck, Fortune, or Really Good Planning?

One of my clients, bless her heart, was a very typical Southern belle, just a wonderful older woman. Before I met her, the person who was handling her money — and notice that I did not saying managing — had risked all of this woman's money in the stock market, and this was too great a risk when what she really needed to be doing was preserving her money. She was almost in her nineties, and her biggest concern was to stay in the retirement community where she was living.

She didn't want to live with her children. She tried living with one daughter and became bored because her daughter had to go to work. She liked being in this community where she was with people her own age: they communicate; they do things together. Her fear was that she was going to run out of money.

So she and I put a plan together to reduce risk and get her out of the market and preserve her money. This plan would take care of her until she was 100, and she understood that if she lived past 100, she would become her daughter's problem.

Now here's the irony. This was in 2008. We

moved her out of the stock market two weeks to the day before the bottom fell out. Was that luck or fortune or really good planning?

I consider it a blessing for both of us. A blessing for her because she tells me every time I see her, "I sleep at night. I don't worry." For me, this blessing is why I do this work. I am able to help people live better.

The principle here is that she didn't belong in the stock market, so it was a great fortune and a blessing for both of us that I pulled her out because I was trying to prevent her from losing everything. All of her resources had been at risk, and if she had lost them, she would never get them back. When you are almost 90 years old, you don't have time to gain your money back from the type loss she could have suffered. If she had lost that money, she would not only have lost her money, she would have lost her independence. She would have lost her dignity.

She was in my office recently. She is still

just as beautiful as she can be with a big smile on her face, and she is still independent. If she had gone through the type of major loss she almost suffered, I don't think she would be here today.

◆　◆　◆

"I Don't Have to Worry"

Right after Christmas one year, I got a call from a client who was in the hospital. He was considering using some of his funds to go overseas to get a particular type of treatment. We talked about where we would take the monies from, and he said to me, "Annalee, you have never let me down." He said, "You've always done exactly what you told me you were going to do, and I want to thank you for that." Of course, that just thrilled me.

The week after, I got a call from his wife; he had passed away that day. What he had said is going to stay in my heart forever. Here was a man who appreciated my honesty and my availability when he needed me to be there for him. He had also said to me that day on the phone, "I know I don't have to worry about my wife. I know that you will take care of her."

For anyone to put that type of trust in me is a great blessing. It also is a tremendous responsibility. I have to take good care of her to make sure that she's going to be okay as time goes on.

♦   ♦   ♦

House Call

I normally don't go to clients' homes, but one of my clients had a stroke and couldn't drive anymore. She asked me to stop by her home so we could discuss a CD that was maturing.

So I stopped at her home, and as I got there, I saw a neighbor was with her. My client was very pale, very shaken. When I asked her what had happened, she told me that she had fallen.

I told the neighbor we had business to do and sat down with my client. I didn't open my folder. We just started talking. She admitted to me for the first time in her life that she was afraid to be alone.

We talked about an hour or hour and a half and never did any business. When I left, I said, "You're going to start getting some phone calls, and I want you to go ahead and talk to these people, let them come in, and let's see what they can do to help you."

One of the things we've done in my community is put together a Senior Alliance comprised of about twenty businesses that have the same attitude we have about serving the community. We all are people who know and trust each other. This is not a referral group. Our members are screened for their honesty, their caring, and their willingness to help people.

In our Senior Alliance, we have an estate attorney. We have a real estate agent and a reverse mortgage specialist. We have a business that does downsizing and restaging. We have a home health care agency, social workers, and a rehab center. We have transportation, long-term care, and Medicare specialists. We even have a final needs planning person. We have pulled together the services that people need as they get older. The moral obligation of the group is to make sure that we are doing the best for the client and that the client is always treated with respect and dignity. When we come across a client who needs assistance, we have an agreement to put each other into action.

So, I came back to my office, pulled my staff together, and told them what was happening with my client. We then mobilized several members of our senior alliance. The home health agency started her on physical therapy;

the homemaker agency now helps her several days a week in her home. The senior real estate specialist went out and consulted with her about selling her home and the consequences of that scenario. The downsizing/restaging specialist talked with her about taking what's in the house and putting it into an assisted living community so that she would have the same comfortable home atmosphere. My business partner and I personally took her to two assisted living facilities and let her meet the managers there. We got them to give her a tour. We had a meal while we were there.

Today, she is still in her home. She's eating, and she's much stronger. She's able to do some walking without the walker. She's got color back in her face. She's got that little twinkle back in her eye. Before, she was scared. She felt defeated. Now she's back to being herself. She has a financial plan, and she's not worried. And thanks to our professional alliance, she knows that when she's ready to move to assisted living, everything is ready and in place.

♦ ♦ ♦

The New Widow

My client was recently widowed, and I could tell as soon as I saw her that she was a scared little mouse. She was very tense; her shoulders were up high and her hands were clenched. You could tell she didn't trust anybody, and she was fearful.

We sat down and just started talking. I told her to ask me whatever she wanted and to tell me how I could best serve her, how I could make life a little bit better for her.

Well, about the same time, Beau, one of my miniature schnauzers, came up, and he put his paws on her. He has a unique way about him when anybody is upset in the office. I don't care where it is, he'll find them and sit there.

The woman asked me if she could hold him, so I picked him up and put him in her lap. She started petting the dog, and it was amazing; her shoulders went down, her hands became relaxed, and she just talked. I found out all the things she was afraid of and the mistakes she was afraid of making. Afterwards, we were able to discuss ways to avoid those mistakes and alleviate her fears.

Like many widows, her first thought was to take her money and pay off the house, but that is not always a good decision. The house can't feed you. The house can't put gas in your car. The house cannot pay for the insurance. If she paid off the house, she would have ended up being property rich and cash poor. Thank goodness she decided against paying off the house because soon afterwards, the housing market dropped. Not two years later, she decided to go live near one of her daughters. If she had all her money tied up in that house, she would have lost $250,000, and it never would have returned.

By selling her house later, and combining that with the other money we had kept aside, she had enough to take care of herself for the rest of her life. If she had lost that initial amount of money, it would have been very difficult for her to have a decent life. She would have been okay, but she would have had to severely cut back on her lifestyle. So working together, we were able to make the best decision we could have made for her.

◆　◆　◆

You Never Know

One of my favorite couples recently came in to see me, and it was obvious that the husband had started developing early Alzheimer's; we thought he would be the one to pass first because his wife was a very vivacious woman.

Ironically, she slipped, fell, hit her head, and

was the one who died first.

Afterwards, the husband had to be moved out of state to live near their son. He now is in one of the best nursing homes in their area, and nobody has to pay for it because he had the money and a long-term care policy. He's getting top-of-the-line care, and nobody has to worry about it. The most rewarding thing for me was getting calls from two of the children thanking us for what we did.

◆　◆　◆

Living Life

I have one client I've worked with for many, many years, and she has referred many, many people to me. She is widowed, and when we met she wasn't quite sure where she should go.

We recently did her review. Through the years, she has spent over $50,000 going on cruises. She has done things she wanted to do while she was healthy enough to do them, and even though she has spent over $50,000 doing what she wanted to do, she is still $59,000 ahead.

What a great comfort it is to be able to tell somebody in their eighties, "You've done all these wonderful things, you did the things you wanted to do, and guess what, we still have every penny you spent plus more."

♦　　♦　　♦

A Younger Woman

I'm working with a young woman who has a three-year-old child. She is very smart and is thinking about preparing for her child's college education. Like many women her age, she says she wants to do all the things that she has read about. Unfortunately, those aren't necessarily the best things for her to be doing. There are many other things she can do that will allow her to plan for her retirement while also planning for her child's college education.

I often find that people get so obsessed with their child's college education that they ruin their own retirement. So we sat, and we looked at the things she could do. She and her husband came in and signed all the paperwork to do what needed to be done. Previously, they were trying to do something before they understood it, and they didn't feel good about it. After looking at and becoming educated on the options available to them, they could see what was actually best for them. Now both feel very comfortable with where they are.

◆　◆　◆

The Importance of Communication

She was a cancer survivor, and a very sweet woman, but she didn't have much money. She was the perfect candidate to do a reverse mortgage. It would have made her life so much easier, but she wouldn't do it. She thought her daughter was returning to Pensacola and would want the house when she died.

For the longest time, whenever I met with her, I'd bring this up again as an option, but she was insistent. Unfortunately, the cancer came back, and soon after the last diagnosis, she passed away.

I went to her funeral and met her lovely daughter. Two months later, I opened the paper and happened to see an ad that read, "Estate sale, home, furnishings, all belongings," and right there on the ad was my client's name!

Sadly enough, the daughter didn't want the house and sold it within two months of my client's passing. I don't know why the daughter sold the house, and I don't blame her for doing so. What bothers me to this day is that my very dear client lived the last couple of years of her life in misery because she didn't have the money she could have had if she had chosen to do a reverse mortgage.

If they will allow it, I try to help clients have discussions with family members so they are not operating on bad assumptions. So often, they don't want their children to know the position they are in. Because of my fiduciary responsibility and the privacy issues involved, I cannot speak with their children on my own. I have to abide by my clients' wishes.

The only time I will do otherwise is when I notice that someone whom I've known for a number of years is slipping mentally or physically, and the children are unaware. At that point, I will call the children and let them know that they may want to get their parent to the doctor. They need to know that something has changed about their parent's well-being, but I cannot call them and talk to them about money unless I have the specific permission of their parent. In my experience, it is best if everyone is upfront and honest about all of their needs and desires—emotional, financial, and physical—and has an opportunity to discuss them.

What to Do Now

Writing this book was a memorable experience for me. I love to teach, so writing a book was a natural step for me to share my mission with the world. I sincerely thank you for investing your time in reading.

I hope that you learned more than financial tips and advice. While my goal was to educate you on financial matters, it was more important to me that you learned who I am. You know by now that I am invested in the lives of my clients. It's critical for you to know me as much as I get to know you. I trust that the stories I've told, and the clients I've introduced you to, gave you a better picture of who I am.

If you identified with something I've taught, or saw yourself in the stories I've shared about real people I've worked with, then I would love to talk with you.

By now, you know my passion is to have a personal connection with my clients. I typically serve clients who are a comfortable drive from our Pensacola, Florida, or Mobile, Alabama, offices. It's wonderful to sit at my table and share a cup of coffee or tea together, but I don't exclusively serve clients in this area. I have clients who live all over the country, so don't exclude yourself if you are not able to meet me face to face. We'll simply get to know each other over the phone, and it will be great to get to know you and serve you (just know the invitation is always open for you to visit me in the office to have that cup of coffee or tea).

Let's begin a conversation by having you call my office at 1-850-437-3127 or toll-free 1-877-860- 7752. When you call, we will set up a time for your first consultation. My staff will tell you how to prepare so that we use our time together wisely.

Why not give yourself the gift of 90 minutes of your time and take care of your financial house? If you don't, it may be taken care of by the government or a member of your family that you might not want in charge.

There are also several ways to learn more about me and learn strategies and options for putting your financial life in order.

You could listen my weekly radio show, "Winning with Annalee," on 1620 AM News Radio Pensacola on Tuesday mornings from 10 to 11 am. You could attend one of the retirement planning classes that I teach at Pensacola State College and even attend one of our Financial Matters presentations that we do for the **Senior Spirit Program** at Sacred Heart Hospital in Pensacola and Mobile every month. We'd love for you to come and learn and get to know us before you make that first appointment!

Right after this chapter, there is a resources section containing useful information, including experts within our **Senior Resource Alliance.** These handpicked people are here to help you when you need it.

Lastly, if you want to smile, go to our website **www.MainstayAdvisors.com,** where you will meet my staff members and our smile committee, Beau, Jolie, and Bella. From there, you can go to our full website at **www.MainstayPensacola.com.**

I look forward to seeing you soon.

Resources

Here is the **Escarosa Senior Alliance** I spoke about earlier in the book. You can find us online at **www.EscarosaAlliance.org.** Our group includes experts in financial services, long-term care, Medicare, reverse mortgages, and non-medical services, such as in-home services for memory-impaired or physically impaired clients.

We also work with continuing care facilities

and those who provide medical-related services like physical therapy to recover from surgery or illness. And when you or a loved one reaches the end of life, we have a wonderful connection with a hospice representative.

The Alliance includes wonderful estate planning attorneys who will give you what you need and not try to make you do something that you don't need. We even have experts who can help you sell your home and downsize to a smaller area.

My goal with the practice and with the alliance is to provide good, honest care and education to the people who need it.

GENERAL HELP

Administration on Aging
www.aoa.gov

National Aging Information Center
www.aoa.gov/naic/

National Institute on Aging
www.nia.nih.gov

Eldercare Locator 1-800-677-1116
www.eldercare.gov

AARP
www.aarp.org

First Gov for Seniors
www.seniors.gov

Social Security Administration
1-800-772-1213
www.ssa.gov

Medicare
1-800-633-4227
www.medicare.gov

Department of Veterans Affairs
www.va.gov

ALZHEIMER'S DISEASE

Alzheimer's Association
800-272-3900
www.alz.org

Alzheimer's Disease Education
and Referral Center
800-438-4380
www.alzheimers.org

CARE GIVING

AARP Caregivers Circle Discussion Board
http://community.aarp.org

Children of Aging Parents 1-800-227-7294
www.caps4caregivers.org

Administration on Aging
www.aoa.dhhs.gov/caregivers

American Association of Homes
and Services for the Aging
www.aahsa.org/public/consumer.htm

National Council on Aging Benefits Check Up
www.benefitscheckup.org

National Association of Professional
Geriatric Care Managers
www.caremanager.org

DRIVING

National Highway Transportation
Safety Administration
www.nhtsa.dot.gov

Driving Safely While Aging Gracefully
www.nhtsa.dot.gov/people/injury/olddrive

Read Your Road
www.ohs.fhwa.dot.gov/outreach/ryr/

Driving Safely While Aging Gracefully
www.nhtsa.dot.gov/people/injury/olddrive/

American Public Transportation Association
www.apta.com

EMPLOYMENT

The Senior Job Bank
www.seniorjobbank.org

Senior Community Service Employment
Program wdsc.doleta.gov/seniors

The National Senior Citizens Education
and Research Center
www.nscerc.org

Experience Works
www.experienceworks.org

AARP Working Options
www.aarp.org/working_options

FINANCIAL HELP

Certified Financial Planner Board of Standards www.cfp-board.org

Consumer Federation of America
www.consumerfed.org

Federal Consumer Information Center
www.pueblo.gsa.gov

American Savings Education Council
www.asec.org

Pension and Welfare Benefits Administration
www.dol.gov/dol/pwba

U.S. Securities and Exchange
www.sec.gov

FLU PREVENTION

Flu Facts for Everyone
www.cdc.gov/nip/flu

Focus on the Flu
www.niaid.nih.gov/newsroom/focuson/flu00/

FRAUD

Federal Trade Commission
www.ftc.gov

National Fraud Information Center
www.fraud.org

U.S. Department of Justice
www.usdoj.gov/criminal/fraud/telemarke

Medicare
www.medicare.gov/FraudAbuse/Overview.asp

Department of Health and Human Services
www.dhhs.gov/progorg/oei/outreach/outre
ach.htm

GRANDPARENTING

Foundation for Grandparenting
www.grandparenting.org

AARP Grandparent Information Center
www.aarp.org/grandparents

Grand Parent Again
www.grandparentagain.com

GrandsPlace
www.grandsplace.com

LEGAL HELP (WILLS, TRUST AND ESTATE)

AARP – Legal Services Network
www.aarp.org/lsn

National Academy of Elder Law Attorneys
www.naela.org/naela/hotlinks.htm

American Bar Association
www.abanet.org/store/order.html

American Academy of Estate Planning Attorneys: www.estateplanforyou.com

Nolo Press self help law center:
www.nolo.com

American Bar Association:
www.abanet.org

MetLife Consumer Education Center:
www.lifeadvice.com

Senior Legal Hotlines
www.legalhotlines.org

ElderLawAnswers.com
www.elderlawanswers.com

PRESCRIPTION DRUGS

Medicare Prescription Drug Assistance
Programs
www.medicare.gov/Prescription/Home.asp

Free/Discounted/Affordable Prescription
Medication
www.makoa.org/freemedicine.htm

RxAssist
www.rxassist.org

WellRxCard
www.wellrxcard.com

National Association of Boards of Pharmacy
complete list of online drugstores
www.nabp.net

Pharmaceutical Research and Manufacturers of America 1-800-762-4636
www.phrma.org

TRICARE Senior Pharmacy Program
www.tricare.osd.mil

AARP Prescription Savings Service
www.aarppharmacy.com

How to Apply to Free Prescription Drug Programs
www.sunflower.org/~cfsdays/freedrug.htm

REVERSE MORTGAGES

National Center for Home Equity Conversion
www.reverse.org
National Reverse Mortgage Lenders Association www.reversemortgage.org

U. S. Department of Housing
and Urban Development
www.hud.gov

SOCIAL SECURITY

Social Security Administration 1-800-772-1213 www.ssa.gov